The Three Lettered Mantra of Rama
for
Rama Jayam - Likhita Japam Mala

Journal for Writing the 3-Lettered Rama Mantra

त्र्यक्षर राम मंत्र
व
राम जयम - लिखित जपम्
राम-नाम लेखन माला

Belongs to _____

Published by: **Rama-Nama Journals**
(an Imprint of e1i1 Corporation)

Title: **The Three Lettered Mantra of Rama, for Rama Jayam - Likhita Japam Mala**
Sub-Title: **Journal for Writing the 3-Lettered Rama Mantra**

Author: **Sushma**

Copyright Notice: **Copyright © e1i1 Corporation © Sushma**
All rights reserved. No part of this publication may be reproduced, distributed, or transmitted in any form or by any means, including photocopying, recording, or other electronic or mechanical methods.

<u>Identifiers</u>
ISBN: **978-1-945739-33-0** (Paperback)

—o—

www.**e1i1**.com -- www.**OnlyRama**.com
email: **e1i1**books**e1i1**@gmail.com

Our books can be bought online, or at Amazon, or any bookstore. If a book is not available at your neighborhood bookstore they will be happy to order it for you. (Certain Hardcover Editions may not be immediately available—we apologize)

Some of our Current/Forthcoming Books are listed below. Please note that this is a partial list and that we are continually adding new books. Please visit www.**e1i1**.com / www.**onlyRama**.com for current offerings.

- **Tulsi Ramayana—The Hindu Bible:** Ramcharitmanas with English Translation & Transliteration
- **Tulsi-Ramayana Rama-Nama Mala (multiple volumes):** Legacy Journals for Writing the Rama Name alongside Tulsidas Ramcharitmanas—contains English Translation & Transliteration, Inspirational Quotes of Hindu saints, and space for you to jot down your spiritual sentiments on a daily basis. Once embellished with your Rama-Namas, these books become priceless treasures which you can present to your loved ones—a true gift of love, labor, caring, wishing, and above all—Devotion.
- **Ramcharitmanas:** Ramayana of Tulsidas with Transliteration (in English)
- **Ramayana, Large**: Tulsi Ramcharitmanas, Hindi only Edition, Large Font and Paper size
- **Ramayana, Medium**: Tulsi Ramcharitmanas, Hindi only Edition, Medium Font and Paper size
- **Ramayana, Small**: Tulsi Ramcharitmanas, Hindi only Edition, Small Font and Paper size
- **Sundarakanda:** The Fifth-Ascent of Tulsi Ramayana
- **RAMA GOD:** In the Beginning - Upanishad Vidya (Know Thyself)
- **Purling Shadows:** And A Dream Called Life - Upanishad Vidya (Know Thyself)
- **Fiery Circle:** Upanishad Vidya (Know Thyself)
- **Rama Hymns:** Hanumān-Chalisa, Rama-Raksha-Stotra, Bhushumdi-Ramayana, Nama-Ramayanam, Rama-Shata-Nama-Stotra, etc. with Transliteration & English Translation
- **Rama Jayam - Likhita Japam Mala alongside Sacred Hindu Texts (several):** Journals for Writing the Rama Name 100,000 Times alongside various Hindu Texts, with English Translation & Transliteration. Embellish these Books with your Rama-Namas and they become transformed into priceless treasures which you can later gift to your loved ones.
- **Rama Jayam - Likhita Japam Mala alongside Rama-Mantras (several):** Journals for Writing the Rama Name alongside the Rama-Mantras from one lettered to thirty-two & others. Embellish these with your Rama-Namas and they become transformed into priceless treasures.

-- On our website may be found links to renditions of Rama Hymns –
-- Rama Mantras/Hymns/Pictures are also available printed on Quality Shirts from Amazon. See our website for details –

rāma-nāma mahimā

As per *Hindu-Darshan* (philosophy), there is just a one-Consciousness which pervades the Universe, with nothing else besides; and the very nature of that consciousness is Bliss. And yet, though our essential nature is rooted in Bliss, still most of us live in misery. Why? Well, according to Tulsīdās, a gemstone is not valued until it is identified by its name. In the same way, the one immortal, true, sentient, complete, and blissful all-pervading Brahmm—persists in bondage and suffering (as the visible woeful creation), until becoming revealed into a definite form and name—energized by the Name 'Rāma'.

Rāma is Bliss. The Rāma-Nāma—Name of Rāma, is the key to that Bliss.

The potency of Rāma-Nāma is unsurpassed in all the four Yugas; the Vedas and other scriptures sing of its glories; and the saints swear by it—especially so in the present Age. In the Kali-Yuga, the chanting of Rāma-Nāma is regarded as most-effective and most-supreme—being that in such iniquitous Times, there is no other easy means of salvation.

The present Kali-Yuga, the Iron-Age, is rightly described as vile and sinful. It is awash with the six Gunas of Māyā: Kāma (Lust), Krodha (Anger), Lobha (Greed), Moha (Infatuation), Mada (Pride) & Mātsarya (Envy)—and here we find our minds sinking in worldliness despite our best intentions. Seemingly none can remain unsullied from the taints of Kali—this appears to be the fait-accompli of the Kali-Yuga—a very sad state indeed. But despair not, for when it comes to attaining salvation, many consider this Kali-Yuga to be the Golden-Age. Yes, Kali-Yuga has this one great blessing: through a very simple expediency—simply by a complete surrender to the Holy Name Rāma—one is able to attain to that very high divine state, that very supreme seat, which sages scarcely attained to even after practicing great penances and sacrifices in former Times.

In the Sata-Yuga, contemplation; in the Tretā, sacrifice; and in the Dwāpar-Yuga worship—these were the appointed propitiations; but in this vile and impure Kali-Yuga—where the soul of man is alike a hapless fish floating in the ocean of sin—in such dreadful times, the Nāma is the only tree of eternal life; and by meditating upon it all the vile commotions become stilled. In these Times neither good deeds, nor piety, nor spiritual wisdom is of any avail—but only the Name of Rāma. The Rāma-Nāma is, as it were, the wisdom and might of Hanumān that exposes and destroys the Kālnemī-like wiles of the wicked world.

Sing the praises of the Lord and remain engaged in *Nāma-Smarana*—is the advice given to us by our saints; the Japa of Rāma-Nāma is the supreme path to salvation—assure our Scriptures; there is no Dharma higher than Nāma-Dharma in this Age—aver the wise. The chanting of Rāma-Nāma is The-One-Supreme-Path to escape the clutches of Kali-Yuga—declares Rāmacharitmānas; in fact it is the one and only Dharma which is easy and feasible given the vicious nature of the present Times.

Well do our scriptures repeatedly assert: In this Kali-Yuga, there is no other means, no other means, no other means of salvation—other than chanting the holy name Rāma, chanting the holy name Rāma, chanting the holy name Rāma.

Talking of the Rāma-Nāma, Tulsīdās says: रा , म are the two most gracious syllables, the eyes as it were of the soul, the miracle charms which satisfy one's every wish, a gain for this world and felicity in the next. These are nectar-like syllables which stand together united, and are most delightful to utter and hear, and easy to remember. Love naturally gets stirred up as we speak these two mystic syllables: syllables which abide together as inseparably as Rāma and Lakshman, or like the duo Nārayana & Nara; syllables which are as intimately connected as the Universal-Soul and the individual-soul; syllables that are preservers of the world and redeemers of the elect; syllables that shine resplendent like two bright jewels on the ears of Bhakti—Beauteous Devotion; syllables that are pure and beneficent as the Sun and the Moon; syllables that are like sweetness and contentment—the inseparable attributes of ambrosia; syllables that are as inseparable as the hovering bee of devout-souls to the lotus of the Supreme-Soul.

Yogis—who are full of dispassion and detached from the world—are able to keep awake in the daylight of wisdom repeating these two syllables of the Name of Rāma, and thus enjoy the incomparable felicity of Brahmm-Rāma—who is incomparable, unspeakable, unmixed with sorrow and void of name and form. *Gyanis*—those who aspire for knowledge—are able to understand all the mysteries by repeating the Name Rāma. *Sadhaks* (Strivers), who repeat the Name Rāma, absorbed in contemplation, become workers of miracles and acquire great mystic powers. They, who repeat it when burdened with affliction, are freed from their troubles and become blissful and content.

There are four kinds of devotees, and all the four are virtuous, sinless, and noble, and all the four—clever as they are—rely upon the Rāma Name. Even those—who are free from all desires and remain ever absorbed in the joy of devotion to Shrī Rāma—throw their heart as fish into the nectarine lake of affection for the Name Rāma.

In all the four ages; in all times, past, present, or future; in the three spheres of earth, heaven and hell—any creature that repeats the name Rāma becomes blessed. The name of Rāma is like the tree of paradise, the centre of all that is good in the world; and whoever meditates upon it verily becomes transformed—from the vile to holy.

As Narasingh was manifested to destroy Hiranyā-kashyap, the enemy of heaven—in order to protect Prahlād—so is राम, the Name of Rāma, for the destruction of the wicked and the protection of the pious.

The chanting of Rāma-Nāma is a direct way to liberation. By repeating this name—whether in joy or in sadness, in activity or in repose—bliss is diffused all around. According to the Vedas, just as the sun dispels the darkness, the chanting of Rāma-Nāma dispels all the evils and obstacles of life. The Rāma Nāma cures agony and showers the blessings of God; all righteous wishes get fulfilled; jealousy and pride disappear; life becomes imbued with satisfaction and peace; all of life's needs fall in place automatically—just like a miracle of nature guiding nature's forces. You may not always get what you want in the exact same form, but the Rāma-Nāma will purify things and bring to you the same needed happiness and bliss in a much more refined and lasting way. Life truly becomes filled with tranquility. With the Rāma-Nāma, an immense sense of spiritual wellbeing is experienced apart from a gain of material happiness.

*If you do not know how to write राम in Sanskrit it is quite easy. Trace the contours 1-2 (which is the sound of **r** in '**r**un'), 3-4 (the sound of **a** in '**a**rk'), 5-6 & 7-8 (the sound **m** in '**m**ust') and lastly make the line 9-10.*

Rāma-Japa—the constant repetition of the Supreme-Mantra 'Rāma'—is usually done mentally, or on a rosary; but there is one extremely efficacious method of this Japa: the Likhita-*Japa*, or the Written-Chant. The practice of writing the Rāma Mantra over and over on paper is called the Likhita-Japa. This written form of Japa is a lasting record of your chant, remaining ever imbued with those holy vibrations, for all times, for the benefit of you and the future generations. In India, as you may know, devotees of God have been chanting the name 'Rāma' राम and writing the Name 'Rāma' राम—pages upon pages of it, running into billions and billions, for ages. Hindu children are taught to write the राम Rāma-Nāma from their childhood.

The Likhit*a* Rāma-Nāma Japa is a powerful and transformative tool. As you write the Rāma-Nāma, all the senses become engaged in the service of the Lord-God, and you find yourself simultaneously chanting and hearing and contemplating on the Lord—everything comes together naturally. This method clears away your thoughts and helps concentrate the entirety of your soul upon the Divine.

Any Japa is beneficial but somehow writing the Rāma-Nāma राम on paper brings up a great singularity of focus within the mind—and the peace of heart which ensues is something which is not so easily achieved with other forms of Japa. The written form of Rāma-Japa is somehow able to engage those parts of our body-mind continuum which other methods can not—and our meditative stance is able to gain much deeper levels thereby.

Although the Rāma-Mantra is the gateway to higher consciousness and spiritual upliftment, but even at such junctures—when you find yourself in odd situations, where all the paths seem blocked—then just walking away from everything and simply writing the Rāma Nāma, will give you a much needed clarity of thought—and a divine inspiration that will show a way out.

The Rāma Nāma is very transformative: with it you gain a balanced progress in your outside world and the inner. Sant Tulsīdās says in Rāmacharitmānas: Place the Rāma-Nāma Jewel at the threshold, and there will be light both inside and out; i.e. a constant chant of the Rāma-Nāma from the mouth—the doorway to the body—will bring you external materialistic wellbeing, and also an inner spiritual wellness—both. Incredibly, with the Rāma-Nāma, you get to have the best of both the worlds.

There is something special that happens when you write the राम Rāma-Nāma. Peace and tranquility surrounds you as you write the Supreme-Mantra. The Rāma-Mantra imparts to you divine strength and great tolerance to withstand the vicissitudes of life. Bright unclouded wisdom illumines your mind. You find yourself in complete surrender to your inner Being. The resonance of God resonates throughout your mind-body continuity. You feel a flux of divine energy resonating within. You get great power and peace in your everyday life. The Japa of Rāma Mantra protects our inner world as well as the outside.

These journals are for performing the written-Japa of the Rāma-Mantras. Please note that at certain places in the Rāma-Rahasya Upanishad, it is advised to do a certain number of Chants following a prescribed method when trying to pursue a special objective—and you are welcome to follow that regimen separately if you so desire; however the focus of this journal is very simple: a simple introduction to the Mantra, and doing a Written-Japa of that Mantra to gain the grace of Lord Shrī Rāma. Rāma is the most gracious forms of the Lord-God, and He gets pleased through the simplest of means.

This journal is for writing the Three-Lettered Rāma-Mantra. A brief introduction of the Mantra is given and it is repeated on every page. A larger Mantra outlines is also printed on each page in case you wish to create a pattern as you write. If you fill this with the Rāma-Mantras using color/size/slant that is different from the outside—then it will also make a large Mantra stand out in the waves of surrounding Rāma-Mantras. Devotees usually make such interesting patterns in their Likhita Japa. Most Devotees will use red ink for writing; some will use different colors to create designs; some will have a special set of pens kept purely for the Likhita in the belief that such implements—that are habitually used for holy tasks—build up energy and holy resonance of their own. There are no hard rules; do what feels natural to you. Also, please feel free to choose any notebook or paper to write upon, not necessarily this Journal.

Please note: if writing the larger Mantras is too whelming for you, you can just embellish these pages with simply the Two-Lettered Mantra राम—the Most Supreme Mantra in existence, so sweet and nectar like, and so simple to chant, mutter, write.

Write the Rāma-Mantra with reverence, every day, preferably at a set time, or as and when possible, in small measures, or copiously—howsoever your situation permits. There are no hard rules, do what feels good to your Soul. The important thing is to engage in the Likhita-Japa. When completed, you could keep the Likhita-Japas in your Worship-Room, preserve them as treasures to pass on to future generations, donate them to Rāma Temples that preserve them, or gift them to your loved ones—who will thereby inculcate crucial values from you and learn the importance of the Rāma-Nāma, and get inspired with Hindu Values, especially so the younger ones.

While writing, focus your mind on the Rāma-Mantra and chant it within. Imagine Sītā-Rāma showering you with their bliss. Try to stay free of distractions, and with time you will find that your mind will take a natural meditative stance while engaged in the written Rāma-Nāma Japa.

Once embellished with your Rāma-Nāmas, these Journals will become priceless treasures which you can present to your loved ones—an unparalleled gift of love, labor, caring, wishing, and above all—Devotion. We wish you a very blissful Rāma-Nāma Japam.

Our following Journals:
Tulsi-Ramayana Rama-Nama Mala (in multiple volumes): Legacy Journals for Writing the Rama Name alongside Full Tulsi Ramayana, are legacy Journals in which you can write down your spiritual sentiments, and the Rāma-Nāma, alongside the printed Tulsi Rāmayana. These Journal-Books contain the original text, transliteration, translation, and space for you to jot down your thoughts and write the Rāma-Nāma. Pages also have inspirational words of Hindu Saint to help guide aspirants on their spiritual journey. You can embellish the entire Tulsi Rāmayana with your Rāma-Nāmas and gift them to your loved ones—a truly unique gift of love, care, labor, and devotion.

Our following Journals:
Rama Jayam - Likhita Japam Mala alongside Sacred Hindu Texts (several)
are Journals for performing the 100,000 Rama-Nama Likhita Japa alongside Sacred Hindu Texts like:
Hanumān Chalisa, Nama Ramayanam, Rama-Ashtottara-Shata-Nama-Valih, Rama-Ashtottara-Shata-Nama-Stotra, Rama Raksha Stotra, Ramashtakam... *(and more on the way)*

the three-lettered mantra of śrī-rāma

Once, the enlightened *Rishis*: Mudgala, Shandilya, Paingala, Bikshu etc.—all distinguished seers who were skilled in philosophy and science, prodigious masters of penance & austerities—accompanied by other ascetics and sages like the Sanaka, as well as many devotees of Lord Vishnu such as Prahalād—approached Shrī Hanumān.

These great masters—who had attained to the pinnacle of their spiritual knowledge and were considered most wise and erudite—had come to Hanumān in order to get access to the highest knowledge; and they said unto Hanumān: "O thou mighty brave Lord; O son-of-the-wind-god, do please teach us: What is that ultimate essence which is known to those who are renowned experts in the knowledge pertaining to Brahmm? What is the basis tenet, the cardinal essence, the substantive edict of the eighteen Puranas, the eighteen sub-Puranas, and the Smritis? The four Vedas and all the scriptures are well known to thee—they have been taught to thee by none other than the sun-god. Thy knowledge is more comprehensive than that of anyone. Oh the valiant brave Hanumān, do please tell: What is the essence of all the great teachings? What is the fundamental knowledge expounded and enunciated by the scriptures?"

And Hanumān replied: "O ye exalted sages, seers, ascetics, and devotees of the Lord! Listen carefully to what I have to say. It has the potential of destroying sin, and rent asunder all fetters of this deluding fearsome Creation. It incorporates the essence of all that's at the heart of our scriptures and metaphysics. The very core of the tenets, axioms and maxims, the greatest principle amongst them, is the principle of Tārak-Brahmm—that form of Brahmm which delivers one from the torments associated with this seemingly endless cycles of births and deaths; which releases the soul from bondages and into complete bliss and felicity. Hear ye all and know: It is Rāma who is the supreme transcendental Brahmm. Rāma is that ultimate '*Tattwa*'—the essence, the fundamental aspect—which thou enquire of and seek. It is Shrī Rāma who is the Tārak Brahmm. Rāma is Brahmm personified, the embodiment of Supreme Consciousness & Bliss; Rāma is Para-Brahmm, the supreme austerity; Rāma is the Ultimate Essence of the Universe—the *Tārak-Brahmm*."

The sages enquired further and Hanumān detailed out to them the various aspects of the divine forms of Shrī Rāma. Those great sages, led by Sanaka, now wished to learn of the Mantras for meditating upon Rāma and said, "Oh thou strong, valiant son of Anjani! Lord Rāma is celebrated as Tārak—the Redeemer, and as Brahmm—the All-Pervading Supreme-Soul. We request thee to please teach to us his Divine Holy Mantras for our welfare—those Mantras through which one can meditate and worship the Tārak-Brahmm Rāma." And Hanumān graciously taught to them the various Mantras of Rāma.

The Two-Lettered Supreme Mantra is राम (**rāma**); and when prefixed with any one of the six Beej-Mantras then we get the Three-Lettered Rāma Mantra.

The six Beej-Mantras are: ॐ ह्रीं श्रीं क्लीं ऐं रां (om hrīṁ śrīṁ klīṁ aiṁ rāṁ)

The Three-Lettered Rāma Mantras are:

ॐ राम	—	om rāma
ह्रीं राम	—	hrīṁ rāma
श्रीं राम	—	śrīṁ rāma
क्लीं राम	—	klīṁ rāma
ऐं राम	—	aiṁ rāma
रां राम	—	rāṁ rāma

These six Three-Lettered Mantras are rife with divine potential and great mystical powers.

Each monosyllable Beej Mantra stands for an element that has gone into creating this Universe; they represent the fundamental constituents which abide as the kernels, or seeds, of Creation. On their own, they encapsulate great mystic powers within themselves; and when used with the Supreme Mantra Rāma—the resultant energy that ensues is colossal.

.:.

ॐ राम is the Three-Lettered-Mantra of Lord-God Rāma.

The attributeless, infinite transcendental Causal-Supreme-Entity—from whom everything has come into existence—is represented by ॐ.

The ॐ refers to Brahmm—the Divine-Entity, the Absolute Supreme-Being—that abides in that innate coiled-up state which is still to become manifest, or evolved. The ॐ represents that Unmanifest-Supreme which is more subtle than space, subtler than the void.

The ॐ is mentioned in the Vedas as one of the names of Rāma—who is the embodiment of Brahmm.

The Japa of ॐ राम is performed with the view of attaining liberation and merging with the Supreme Absolute; it is for the purpose of finding the Ultimate-Reality; it gives the Jiva that everlasting peace of soul which is known as Nirvana.

∴

ह्रीं राम is the Three-Lettered-Mantra of Lord-God Rāma.

The monosyllable Beej Mantra ह्रीं stands for the Māyā-Shakti—the divine play and cosmic energy—by dint of which this Universe has come about.

This Universe is full of diverse names and forms, although at its very core everything abides as a single Non-Dual-Consciousness; and what makes that wonder possible is known as Māyā; and ह्रीं is the monosyllable sound of that wonderful Cosmic Power.

Having obscured the real nature of Jiva, Māyā is considered to be magical or delusional—it causes the Jiva to persist stupefied and remain in bondages, forgetting his true nature. The Beej Mantra ह्रीं is therefore used to propitiate Māyā—to win her over and get out of the thralldoms of Māyā.

The Japa of ह्रीं राम enables the aspirant to overcome delusions and the attendant problems of Māyā—those that cause hurdles in spiritual progress; the Japa of ह्रीं राम is for purpose of finding deliverance from this delusional world and attaining to peace.

∴

श्री राम is the Three-Lettered-Mantra of Lord-God Rāma.

The monosyllable Beej Mantra श्री stands for Rāma's consort Shrī Sītā—who is Lakshmī Incarnate—the bestower of opulence & riches.

श्री is representative of richness, plethora, magnificence, opulence, wealth, prosperity, splendor, glory, fame, goodness, well-being. One who aspires for a worldly well-being, through the benign grace of Lord-God Sītā-Rāma, should perform the Japa of श्री राम in order to please them and gain auspiciousness in life.

∴

क्लीं राम is the Three-Lettered-Mantra of Lord-God Rāma.

The monosyllable Beej Mantra क्लीं stands for Kamadev, the cosmic force which abides behind natural desires & passions.

One who seeks worldly pleasures through the benign favor of the Lord-God should perform the Japa of क्लीं राम.

.:.

ऐं राम is the Three-Lettered-Mantra of Lord-God Rāma.

The monosyllable Beej Mantra ऐं stands for the Vāka-Shaktī, the energy which is inherent in speech, knowledge, wisdom, learning. Goddess Saraswatī—the deity of arts, knowledge, sciences—abides in ऐं, the element which represents the faculties of speech, wisdom, knowledge.

The Japa of ऐं राम enables the aspirant to acquire the highest learning and wisdom, and also the power of articulation.

.:.

रां राम is the Three-Lettered Mantra of Lord-God Rāma. This most illustrious Mantra is considered to be the King of Mantras.

The monosyllable रां is the One-Lettered Mantra of Rāma called the Tārak-Beej; it is radiant, energetic, glorious and dynamic as the Fire. रां stands for the fire-element as well as for Shrī Rāma.

The Rishī (patron sage) of the Three-Lettered Rāma-Mantra रां राम is Brahammā, the Creator; the chamda (छंद—meter or poetic style) is the Gayatrī, and Rāma Himself is the Devatā (the patron deity) of the Mantra.

Through the Japa of रां राम, one obtains ultimate liberation and deliverance from this world of delusions; through it the Jiva finally gets emancipation & salvation—the final rest.

.:.

To sum up, the Beej-Mantras are suffixed with the राम Mantra to attain a multiplier effect and enhance the powers of those Mantras. These Three-Lettered Rāma-Mantras are replete with powers to bless the seeker with fulfillment of wishes of their choosing. The Rāma-Mantra राम is just like *Kalpa-Vriksha*, the wish-fulfilling Tree of Paradise; all who take its shelter in complete faith obtain great blessings and acquire whatever they seek.

Let us remember: The Key to Bliss is in Rāma राम.

O my mind, ever meditate on Rāma, the Supreme Being who manifested Himself upon Earth to sport with His devotees, who dwells here for our sake, who fulfills our aspirations. Ever remain in remembrance of Rāma राम—who is eternal and infinite, who is the embodiment of light, who is the cosmic Consciousness that pervades throughout Creation as the Only-Reality, who is the self-illuminated Absolute-Being who shines of His own splendor.

Those who affectionately meditate upon राम, go beyond sin; they go beyond sorrows and remain immersed in the rapture of राम.

obeisance to śrī-rāma

सीतारामगुणग्रामपुण्यारण्यविहारिणौ ।
sītārāmaguṇagrāmapuṇyāraṇyavihāriṇau,
वन्दे विशुद्धविज्ञानौ कवीश्वरकपीश्वरौ ॥४॥
vande viśuddhavijñānau kavīśvarakapīśvarau. 4.

I reverence the king of bards (Vālmikī) and the king of monkeys (Hanumān), of pure intelligence, who ever linger with delight in the holy woods in the shape of glories of Sītā-Rāma.

उद्भवस्थितिसंहारकारिणीं क्लेशहारिणीम् ।
udbhavasthitisaṁhārakāriṇīṁ kleśahāriṇīm,
सर्वश्रेयस्करीं सीतां नतोऽहं रामवल्लभाम् ॥५॥
sarvaśreyaskarīṁ sītāṁ nato'haṁ rāmavallabhām. 5.

I bow to Sītā, the beloved consort of Rāma; the responsible cause of creation, sustenance and dissolution of the universe; who removes afflictions and begets all blessings.

यन्मायावशवर्त्ति विश्वमखिलं ब्रह्मादिदेवासुरा
yanmāyāvaśavartti viśvamakhilaṁ brahmādidevāsurā
यत्सत्त्वादमृषैव भाति सकलं रज्जौ यथाहेर्भ्रमः ।
yatsattvādamṛṣaiva bhāti sakalaṁ rajjau yathāherbhramaḥ,
यत्पादप्लवमेकमेव हि भवाम्भोधेस्तितीर्षावतां
yatpādaplavamekameva hi bhavāmbhodhestitīrṣāvatāṁ
वन्देऽहं तमशेषकारणपरं रामाख्यमीशं हरिम् ॥६॥
vande'haṁ tamaśeṣakāraṇaparaṁ rāmākhyamīśaṁ harim. 6.

I reverence Lord Harī, known by the name of Shrī Rāma; the Supreme causative Cause; whose Māyā holds sway over the entire world, upon every being and supernatural beings from Brahammā downwards; whose presence lends positive reality to the world of appearances—even as the false notion of a serpent is entertained with reference to a rope; and whose feet are the only bark for those eager to cross this ocean of mundane existence.

∴

[Above adapted from: Tulsi-Ramayana--the Hindu Bible]

ॐ राम ॐ राम ॐ राम ॐ राम ॐ राम ॐ राम ॐ राम

ॐ राम   ॐ राम   ॐ राम   ॐ राम   ॐ राम   ॐ राम   ॐ राम

ॐ

राम

Today's Date: _____

ॐ राम   ॐ राम   ॐ राम   ॐ राम   ॐ राम   ॐ राम   ॐ राम

ॐ

राम

_____ Today's Date

ॐ राम   ॐ राम   ॐ राम   ॐ राम   ॐ राम   ॐ राम   ॐ राम

ॐ

राम

Today's Date : _____

ही राम   ही राम   ही राम   ही राम   ही राम   ही राम   ही राम

श्री राम श्री राम श्री राम श्री राम श्री राम श्री राम श्री राम

क्रीं राम   क्रीं राम   क्रीं राम   क्रीं राम   क्रीं राम   क्रीं राम   क्रीं राम

क्लीं राम क्लीं राम क्लीं राम क्लीं राम क्लीं राम क्लीं राम क्लीं राम

क्लीं

राम

Today's Date : _____

ऐं राम ऐं राम ऐं राम ऐं राम ऐं राम ऐं राम ऐं राम

ऐं राम   ऐं राम   ऐं राम   ऐं राम   ऐं राम   ऐं राम   ऐं राम

ऐं

राम

रां राम　रां राम　रां राम　रां राम　रां राम　रां राम　रां राम

रां राम   रां राम   रां राम   रां राम   रां राम   रां राम   रां राम

रां

राम

रां राम	रां राम	रां राम	रां राम	रां राम	रां राम	रां राम

रां राम　　रां राम　　रां राम　　रां राम　　रां राम　　रां राम　　रां राम

रां

राम

ॐ राम ॐ राम ॐ राम ॐ राम ॐ राम ॐ राम ॐ राम

ॐ राम　　ॐ राम　　ॐ राम　　ॐ राम　　ॐ राम　　ॐ राम　　ॐ राम

ॐ

राम

Today's Date : _____

ॐ राम　ॐ राम　ॐ राम　ॐ राम　ॐ राम　ॐ राम　ॐ राम

ॐ राम	ॐ राम	ॐ राम	ॐ राम	ॐ राम	ॐ राम	ॐ राम

ॐ

राम

Today's Date : _____

हीं राम हीं राम हीं राम हीं राम हीं राम हीं राम हीं राम

ह्रीं राम ह्रीं राम ह्रीं राम ह्रीं राम ह्रीं राम ह्रीं राम ह्रीं राम

ह्रीं

राम

श्री राम   श्री राम   श्री राम   श्री राम   श्री राम   श्री राम   श्री राम

श्री

राम

श्री राम   श्री राम   श्री राम   श्री राम   श्री राम   श्री राम   श्री राम

श्री

राम

क्ष्रीं राम क्ष्रीं राम क्ष्रीं राम क्ष्रीं राम क्ष्रीं राम क्ष्रीं राम क्ष्रीं राम

क्ष्रीं

राम

ऐं राम ऐं राम ऐं राम ऐं राम ऐं राम ऐं राम ऐं राम

ऐं राम　　ऐं राम　　ऐं राम　　ऐं राम　　ऐं राम　　ऐं राम　　ऐं राम

ऐं राम

| रां राम | रां राम | रां राम | रां राम | रां राम | रां राम | रां राम |

रां राम   रां राम   रां राम   रां राम   रां राम   रां राम   रां राम

रां राम   रां राम   रां राम   रां राम   रां राम   रां राम   रां राम

रां राम   रां राम   रां राम   रां राम   रां राम   रां राम   रां राम

रां

राम

ॐ राम ॐ राम ॐ राम ॐ राम ॐ राम ॐ राम ॐ राम

ॐ राम ॐ राम ॐ राम ॐ राम ॐ राम ॐ राम ॐ राम

ॐ

राम

Today's Date : _____

ॐ राम   ॐ राम   ॐ राम   ॐ राम   ॐ राम   ॐ राम   ॐ राम

ॐ राम ॐ राम ॐ राम ॐ राम ॐ राम ॐ राम ॐ राम

ॐ

राम

Today's Date : _____

हीं राम हीं राम हीं राम हीं राम हीं राम हीं राम हीं राम

ही राम　　ही राम　　ही राम　　ही राम　　ही राम　　ही राम　　ही राम

हों

राम

Today's Date : _____

श्री राम श्री राम श्री राम श्री राम श्री राम श्री राम श्री राम

श्री

राम

श्री राम   श्री राम   श्री राम   श्री राम   श्री राम   श्री राम   श्री राम

श्री राम

क्रीं राम   क्रीं राम   क्रीं राम   क्रीं राम   क्रीं राम   क्रीं राम   क्रीं राम

क्षी राम   क्षी राम   क्षी राम   क्षी राम   क्षी राम   क्षी राम   क्षी राम

क्षों

राम

ऐं राम   ऐं राम   ऐं राम   ऐं राम   ऐं राम   ऐं राम   ऐं राम

ऐं

राम

रां राम   रां राम   रां राम   रां राम   रां राम   रां राम   रां राम

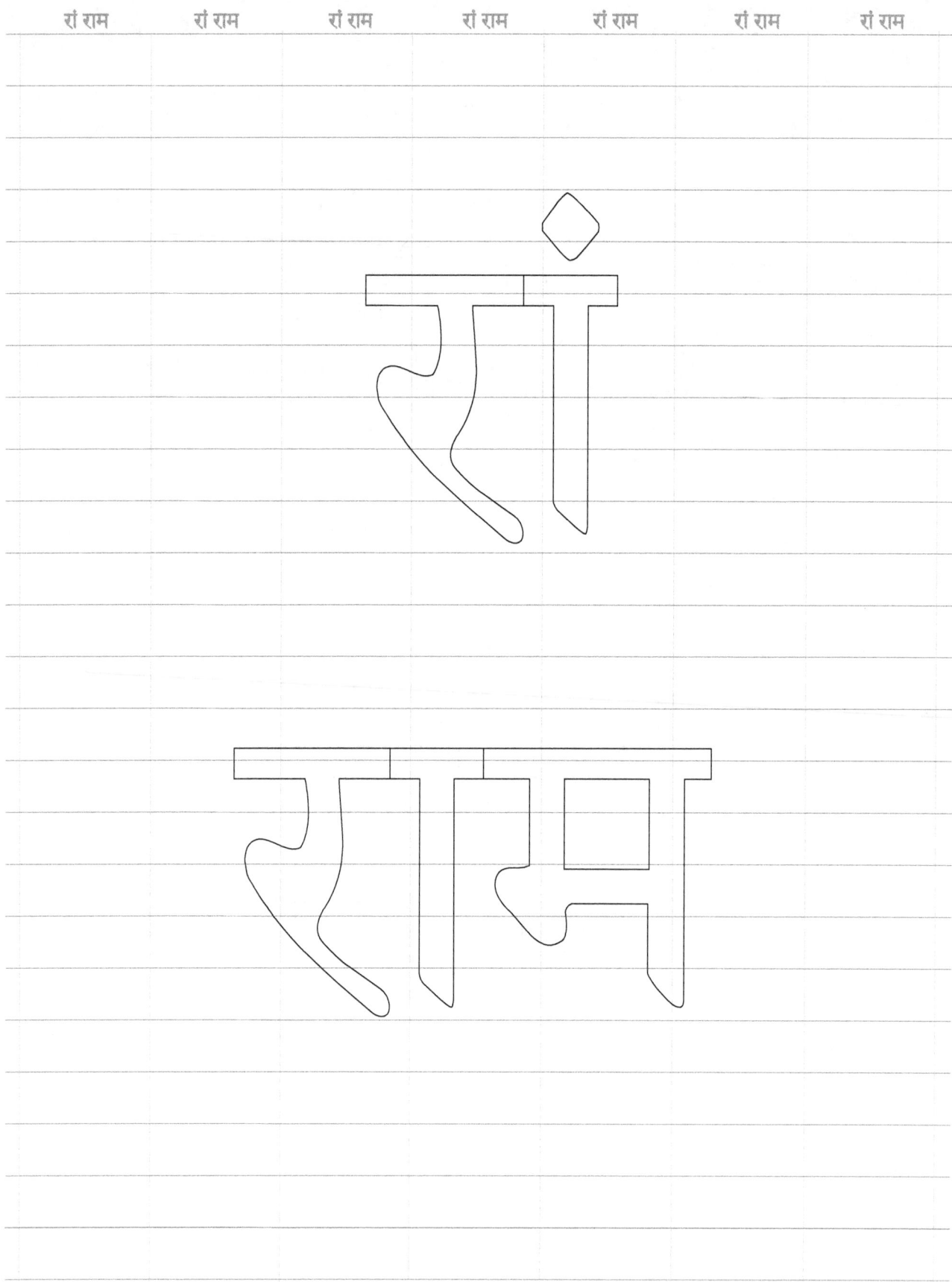

रां राम   रां राम   रां राम   रां राम   रां राम   रां राम   रां राम

रां

राम

रां राम रां राम रां राम रां राम रां राम रां राम रां राम

रां राम रां राम रां राम रां राम रां राम रां राम रां राम

रां

राम

ॐ राम ॐ राम ॐ राम ॐ राम ॐ राम ॐ राम ॐ राम

ॐ

राम

Today's Date : _____

ॐ राम ॐ राम ॐ राम ॐ राम ॐ राम ॐ राम ॐ राम

ॐ राम ॐ राम ॐ राम ॐ राम ॐ राम ॐ राम ॐ राम

Today's Date : _____

| हीं राम | हीं राम | हीं राम | हीं राम | हीं राम | हीं राम | हीं राम |

हों

राम

श्री राम श्री राम श्री राम श्री राम श्री राम श्री राम श्री राम

श्री राम   श्री राम   श्री राम   श्री राम   श्री राम   श्री राम   श्री राम

श्री

राम

क्रीं राम क्रीं राम क्रीं राम क्रीं राम क्रीं राम क्रीं राम क्रीं राम

क्रीं राम   क्रीं राम   क्रीं राम   क्रीं राम   क्रीं राम   क्रीं राम   क्रीं राम

क्लीं राम

ऐं राम ऐं राम ऐं राम ऐं राम ऐं राम ऐं राम ऐं राम

ऐं राम   ऐं राम   ऐं राम   ऐं राम   ऐं राम   ऐं राम   ऐं राम

ऐं

राम

रां राम　रां राम　रां राम　रां राम　रां राम　रां राम　रां राम

रां राम   रां राम   रां राम   रां राम   रां राम   रां राम   रां राम

रां

राम

रां राम   रां राम   रां राम   रां राम   रां राम   रां राम   रां राम

रां राम   रां राम   रां राम   रां राम   रां राम   रां राम   रां राम

ॐ राम   ॐ राम   ॐ राम   ॐ राम   ॐ राम   ॐ राम   ॐ राम

ॐ राम　　ॐ राम　　ॐ राम　　ॐ राम　　ॐ राम　　ॐ राम　　ॐ राम

ॐ

राम

Today's Date : _____

ॐ राम ॐ राम ॐ राम ॐ राम ॐ राम ॐ राम ॐ राम

ॐ

राम

Today's Date : _____

ह्रीं राम ह्रीं राम ह्रीं राम ह्रीं राम ह्रीं राम ह्रीं राम

हीं राम   हीं राम   हीं राम   हीं राम   हीं राम   हीं राम   हीं राम

हीं राम

| श्री राम | श्री राम | श्री राम | श्री राम | श्री राम | श्री राम | श्री राम |

श्री

राम

श्री राम श्री राम श्री राम श्री राम श्री राम श्री राम श्री राम

श्री

राम

क्रीं राम　क्रीं राम　क्रीं राम　क्रीं राम　क्रीं राम　क्रीं राम　क्रीं राम

क्रीं राम   क्रीं राम   क्रीं राम   क्रीं राम   क्रीं राम   क्रीं राम   क्रीं राम

क्रीं

राम

ऐं राम ऐं राम ऐं राम ऐं राम ऐं राम ऐं राम ऐं राम

ऐं राम　　ऐं राम　　ऐं राम　　ऐं राम　　ऐं राम　　ऐं राम　　ऐं राम

ऐं

राम

रां राम   रां राम   रां राम   रां राम   रां राम   रां राम   रां राम

रां राम　　रां राम　　रां राम　　रां राम　　रां राम　　रां राम　　रां राम

रां

राम

रां राम रां राम रां राम रां राम रां राम रां राम रां राम

रां राम   रां राम   रां राम   रां राम   रां राम   रां राम   रां राम

रां

राम

ॐ राम　　ॐ राम　　ॐ राम　　ॐ राम　　ॐ राम　　ॐ राम　　ॐ राम

ॐ राम ॐ राम ॐ राम ॐ राम ॐ राम ॐ राम ॐ राम

ॐ

राम

Today's Date : _____

ॐ राम   ॐ राम   ॐ राम   ॐ राम   ॐ राम   ॐ राम   ॐ राम

ॐ

राम

Today's Date : _____

ही राम ही राम ही राम ही राम ही राम ही राम ही राम

96

ही राम   ही राम   ही राम   ही राम   ही राम   ही राम   ही राम

हों

राम

Today's Date : _____

श्री राम   श्री राम   श्री राम   श्री राम   श्री राम   श्री राम   श्री राम

श्री

राम

क्रीं राम क्रीं राम क्रीं राम क्रीं राम क्रीं राम क्रीं राम क्रीं राम

क्रीं

राम

ऐं राम ऐं राम ऐं राम ऐं राम ऐं राम ऐं राम ऐं राम

ऐं राम   ऐं राम   ऐं राम   ऐं राम   ऐं राम   ऐं राम   ऐं राम

ऐं

राम

रां राम　रां राम　रां राम　रां राम　रां राम　रां राम　रां राम

| रां राम | रां राम | रां राम | रां राम | रां राम | रां राम | रां राम |

रां

राम

रां राम   रां राम   रां राम   रां राम   रां राम   रां राम   रां राम

रां राम रां राम रां राम रां राम रां राम रां राम रां राम

www.ingramcontent.com/pod-product-compliance
Lightning Source LLC
Chambersburg PA
CBHW051754100526
44591CB00017B/2696